Friendly Habits

by Tekla White

illustrated by Beata Spurza

MODERN CURRICULUM PRESS

Pearson Learning Group

NARRATOR 1: Rabbit and Monkey were best friends. They played every day. When it was hot, they either swam across the river or they rested under a tree.

NARRATOR 2: Rabbit and Monkey never sat still. Monkey scratched and scratched all the time. Rabbit's nose and ears wiggled.

RABBIT: Stop scratching!

MONKEY: But there are bugs! I scratch so they will not bite me. But I can stop if I try. Besides, you have bad habits too.

RABBIT: I have to wiggle my
nose and ears. That way I can
tell if anyone is close by. I can
stop if I try.

MONKEY: I say you can't stop.

RABBIT: I say I can. But you can't.

NARRATOR 1: Rabbit and Monkey were not acting like friends. All the animals came toward them to see what was going on.

NARRATOR 2: The birds in the trees said Monkey was right. The animals on the ground said Rabbit was right. All across the forest, they all talked at once.

Elephant: Stop! Only one animal should talk at a time.

Crocodile: I can stop bad habits and noise. I'll open my mouth. You jump in. Then there will be no Rabbit, no Monkey, and no bad habits.

RABBIT AND MONKEY: No thanks.
We will find another way.

MONKEY: Let's have a contest. I'll show you that I can sit still longer than you.

RABBIT: No, I can sit still longer. You will see.

NARRATOR 1: Time went by.

RABBIT: I have to wiggle.

MOUSE: Sit still!

MONKEY: I have to scratch.

PARROT: Don't move!

RABBIT: I'll act out a story to make the time go faster. Here is my story. Something came toward me. I sniffed to the right. I sniffed to the left. Then I hopped away.

MONKEY: I'll act out a story too. My friend dumped a basket of nuts on me. Nuts hit me here, here, and here.

RABBIT: You told that story so you could scratch. It was a trick!

MONKEY: You told your story so you could wiggle your nose. You tricked me too!

NARRATOR 1: Then Rabbit and
   Monkey laughed. They learned
   that habits are not easy to change.
NARRATOR 2: Monkey still scratches.
   Rabbit still wiggles. But they are
   good friends anyway.